I0201844

Now and Zen

teachings of a reluctant master

Now and Zen: teachings of a reluctant master
ISBN 978-960-7395-06-1

©2013 Angelos Bakas | angelos.bakas@gmail.com

ANGELOS BAKAS

Now and Zen

teachings of a reluctant master

2013

Dedicated to the memory of my spiritual brother Adriaan the Dutch, also known as Manolios the gardener and Andreas the shepherd, who left this world as a monk in a Mount Athos monastery.

Now is all there is and it doesn't even exist

Contents

I first met the master while I was contemplating a two–day crossing of a thick and bushy forest, over uncertain paths where it would be very easy for some-one new to these territories, like me, to get hopelessly lost. Therefore, when this stranger appeared with the intention of crossing the forest I asked to tag along and he accepted. He knew the way well and we covered a fair distance before nightfall. The next day we would be out of the woods. We made beds for the night and lay down to sleep. I woke up in the middle of the night feeling terribly thirsty. I reached for my canteen only to find that the lid had not been screwed on properly and all my water had spilled to the ground. I was desperate for some water so I sneaked up to the stranger's belong-ings; I took his flask and drank heartily.

Early the next day we came out of the woods and soon we would each go our way. About to part, the stranger takes his water flask and offers it to me as a present.

"Why do you give me your flask?", I asked.

"Because you obviously enjoy drinking from it", replied the stranger, "when all the time there was a rivulet of clear water running along our path behind the bushes. Where do you think I filled my flask again after you drank it dry?"

I then realised that indeed the flask was full of water.

The stranger shook his head and turned to leave.

"So long, now", he said and waved a hand behind him.

I decided to follow him for a while.

The unploughed field

"Master", I asked, "why do we always walk on the paths around the fields and we don't go through them? They have only just been ploughed and we will not harm any plants. It would save us a lot of walking."

As always, the master took a little time to think about it. "The fields", he finally replied, "though ploughed, remain ignorant and it is not good for us to walk on ignorance."

"What could a ploughed field possibly be ignorant of?", I asked again, sounding very perplexed. The master paused and looked around again at the fields.

"These fields", he said, "do not know that a few months from now we will be eating the seeds that will grow here. This path, however", he said pointing in front of us, "this part of the field, has acquired some knowledge simply by being unploughed, so we are going to walk on it."

The initiated

The master travelled often, and I went with him in some of his travels. Once, we were sitting outside a tavern at the edge of a small town, waiting for a bus that was already a day late, when two young men approached us respectfully and asked whether we knew of a wise man who they heard was visiting their town. They mentioned the name of the wise man and it was the name of the master. Obviously, they did not know what he looked like and I was ready to tell them to look no further, when the master turned and pointed to an alleyway leading to the centre of the town. "He went that way", he said. They thanked us and hurried down the alley. Our bus finally came and soon we were out of the town.

"Why did you have to hide the fact that you were who they were looking for?", I asked, taken somewhat aback by his action.

"My friend", said the master, "it was clear that those boys have had extensive training in spiritual obedience. I was definitely not who they were looking for!"

The peak

Once, the master took me on a trip through dangerous territory, to an ancient monastery, which had been abandoned because of border conflicts, after hundreds of years of spiritual achievements. It was a huge construction and it must have exerted great influence over the area in older times. I asked the master whether he knew how many monks lived in the monastery at its peak. The master thought for a while.

"This monastery came to house up to five thousand monks at some time", he said, "but at its peak it had only five — the master and his four disciples who built here the first shrine."

Choosing

The master barely tolerated being called 'master', let alone 'guru' or 'sage' or any such names. If anyone came to him and said "teach me", he would retort "teach yourself" and dismiss him immediately. The few people who followed him, had come to him mostly by accident, much like I had. However, when I asked him once why he avoided choosing his disciples, all he said was: "Who says I do?"

True wisdom

"A few years ago", said the master, "I visited a small monastery, whose master, rumour had it, was a man of great wisdom. When I arrived, all the monks were sitting quietly in the yard, practicing the art of doing nothing. After I bowed many times to get their attention, I asked who the master was. Immediately, one of the monks replied: 'I am'. I bowed again many times and I left the yard. I went into the garden, where I spoke with the man who was tending the vegetables. He was a very enlightened person."

The master took a sip from his tea. "It's never too difficult", he concluded, "to see where true wisdom lies."

Boredom

We were waiting and waiting for a bus that wouldn't come. "I'm bored", I murmured to myself and the master immediately hit me over the head with his staff. "What do you feel now?", he asked. "Pain", I said, frowning and rubbing my head. "Good!", he said. "Pain is better than boredom."

Issues

There were things the master would rarely or never talk about. Food, for example, was never an issue, since he only eat locally produced vegetables and fruit, seeds and nuts, always raw and in small quantities. Money was also never discussed, since the master did not have or need any. At the places where he was known as a doctor, the impoverished patients not only didn't pay a penny, but they were also loaded with the offerings of the richer patients when they departed. Sex, both the gender and the act, was of absolutely no interest to him. Race, religion or social status, were also ignored when it came to whom he was keeping company with. He seemed indifferent to most of the things valued by most people, but there was something that seemed to absorb all of his interest: how people constructed their beliefs and how they shaped their faith. About these matters, the master was in constant wonder.

Life and death

A visitor asked the master: "What is death?"
"I don't know", said the master. "I'm still alive."
"Then, master, tell me please, what is life?", asked again the visitor.
"I don't know", said again the master. "I'm still in it!"

A virtue

"Master, why do we have food taboos?"

"Because we have plenty to eat."

"Then, why do we not accept money?"

"Because we don't need any."

"So, is there no virtue connected to these habits?"

"Of course there is! It's called common sense!"

Moving

"Master, you don't really like staying put in one place, do you?", I asked once.

"Of course I do!", he replied.

"But, we are constantly moving from one place to the other."

"Oh. I see what you mean", said the master. "Yes. I often move, but only on the outside. On the inside I am always in one place, and immovably so."

Rituals

The master did not follow any particular rituals, except two, which he followed almost religiously: every morning he saluted excitedly towards the sun, and every night he would shout his appreciation and thanks to the stars and beyond, for everything given to him that day.

Family

I was always amazed by the vitality and the magnetic personality of the master, and once, I dared ask him whether he had ever considered raising a family. He laughed and laughed and laughed, until there were tears squirting out of his eyes. He then appeared as if he had just realised that it was a question meant in all seriousness and stopped, only to start laughing again uncontrollably. Finally, exhausted but still highly amused, he reached and picked up the teapot. "Now, stop asking questions that are only fit for a midwife and go make some tea for us", he said.

Language

The master's teachings did not follow any particular programme nor was there any curriculum that I was aware of. Being with him was enough most of the time, because his actions said more about the path he was following than all his words put together. He never much liked that I was constantly writing in my notebook, and insisted that I first meditate on my thoughts before I commit them to paper, because, as he put it, language doesn't describe the world; it creates it!

Mirrors

There were no mirrors in the house of the master, except for a small, round one, stashed away in a box, along with some very basic tools.
"There's really nothing to fix on the outside of a person", the master would say when asked about it. "It's a mirror for the inside that we need."

Meditation

"Today", said the master, "I want you to meditate with this apple until you feel that you have embodied it completely and experienced all of its characteristics. We will talk about it when I come back."

The master left and I started observing the apple, trying to get a deep sense of its aroma, its taste, its colour, trying to remove the barriers to its inner meaning. After some time, I tried to visualise the apple with eyes shut, but my attention kept slipping and I started murmuring a mantram to help me concentrate, to no avail. When the master returned a few hours later, I was still sitting in front of the apple, suffering from a mild headache.

"I failed", I said as soon as I saw him. "I failed miserably."

"Of course you did", said the master and laughed. "My instructions were clear: I asked you to meditate *with* it, not *on* it. You should have eaten the apple, albeit slowly. Didn't you become hungry watching it?"

"Yes! I did! Very! But you didn't explicitly say 'eat it'; you said I should only meditate with it!", I said feeling cheated, and not a little stupid.

"If eating is not meditation", said the master calmly, "then we are nothing more than two–legged omnivores."

25

Professional devotion

One evening the master started telling a story:

A travelling con man was making a fair living posing as a healer. He would visit remote villages and settlements, where he would examine the sick for any payment they could afford. Some success was necessary and he was doing his best to make his patients feel better, using quasi-religious mumbo jumbo, some dubious medicine, and a lot of common sense.

He was a good professional, though, and highly devoted to his art. The con business is very tough and fiercely competitive. He had to be the best to be on top. He started acquiring some real knowledge about the herbs and minerals used in medicine, and tried hard to find what really ails man.

As was to be expected, his con business became very successful and he became a celebrated figure in the world of con artists. He also became a tremendous doctor, though he would never admit to that. To him, it was all a successful con.

"This man was my first master", he said and poured tea for everyone.

The lesser evil

The master had declined many positions of honour in his life, and absolutely refused to be awarded any recognitions by any authority and for any reason. I was, therefore, quite surprised when he accepted to be honoured in a public ceremony at the nearby monastery, for his services as a doctor. I asked him what had made him change his mind about accepting honours and appearing in public ceremonies. He thought for a while. "This strategy has served me well for quite some time", he said, "but now I am in danger of being famous for avoiding fame. Accepting some fame for something I actually do, is the lesser evil."

The real master

When we travelled with the master, we often visited small monasteries, however remote or hard to get to. There, he would always ask to see the master, and when received, we would drink some tea and have a light conversation. After that, we would leave the monastery immediately, even if it meant that we would rest for the night in the wilderness. In one monastery, though, when we asked to see the master, they took us to their shrine and showed us the statue of their god.

There, we stayed for a while.

Plans

We were walking on a wide dirt road for about an hour and all the time the master had his eyes on the ground and he must have been lost in obscure thoughts, because his walk seemed unsteady and uneven. I asked him what he was thinking about and he said he was planning ahead. This was very strange coming from the master, who rarely made plans beyond the current day. I asked him what he was planning. "I plan where I will put my foot next", he said. "This place is crawling with little bugs and I try not to step on any of them."

Dilemmas

The master always seemed to know where he was going, even when we travelled through unknown areas. Once, at a crossroad, I stopped and looked around. "Which road should we take, master?", I asked. "Keep walking", he said, "and ponder how your mind tries to create a dilemma out of a simple situation."

Fame

In our travels, the master often offered his services as a doctor and pharmacist for free, in temples or in village squares. He would work for two days and two nights virtually non-stop, but always on the third day his things were packed and he was ready for departure. "Let's get out of here pretty quick", he would say, "or else we will be rich and famous before we know it."

Mean spirits

The master had great affection for every living thing. Once, a well–to–do visitor who claimed he was practicing zen, brought him a bonzai tree as a present. He went on and on about the years and the concentration demanded for the creation of such a beautiful thing.

When the visitor left, the master took the bonzai tree to his study and meditated on it for three days. When he finally came out, he told us that it was a mean spirit that had created this thing and that we should help the tree get rid of it.

Indeed, year by year, the little bonzai was nurtured back to being a full–blown tree.

Life

I wanted to cut a branch from a tree, to make a staff for our long hikes on the hills, but the master held me gently back. "Everything has been given us", he said, "but nothing that lives is there for us to simply take. Why don't you look for a branch that is already on the ground?"

Let be

The master liked everything in nature as it was. He tended a garden and grew some vegetables, with as little intervention as possible in what grows and what not. One day, a student of zen meditation came and started talking about the art of ikebana and how selecting and arranging flowers and other bits of plants helped him meditate. When he offered to show us how, the master politely declined. "I prefer to let flowers die in their beds", he said.

Religion

In matters of religion, the master was pretty clear: "Whatever can summon man's faith", he would say, "has to be taken extremely seriously."

The cure

The master was an excellent doctor and pharmacist, and sometimes people would come to him, even from afar, for remedies and cures. Once, when he was seeing a middle–aged woman patient from a nearby village, he took me aside and asked me to prepare a particular medicine and mix it in a sweet drink. He insisted the woman should remain unaware of this action. I proceeded with the preparation of the mixture, when I heard loud prayers and incantations from the master's study. This went on and on and stopped just as I was placing the refreshment containing the woman's medicine on a tray. When I entered the study, I noticed various religious artifacts lying on the table, while some incense was still burning in a holder. They were both drenched in sweat and looked exhausted. The woman took the drink thankfully and drank the sweet potion to a drop. She then stood, bent and kissed the master's hand and walked out of the study.

I stood there saying nothing. After a while, the master turned and looked me straight in the eyes. "The medicine will work, whether she knows that she took it or not", he said. "But if something is going to cure her affliction, that's her faith, so, please, don't look at me like that."

Miracles

A visitor came one day and told us excitedly about the Archpriest who had come from the capital to the nearby monastery to perform some sacred ritual, whereby he walked on the surface of the water in a small pond. "Was it a miracle?", the visitor wanted to know. "Of course it's a miracle", said the master, "only, it's a small one. Today I saw a woman giving birth to twin babies, a boy and a girl, and that's a miracle that beats walking on water anytime."

Paradise

Some student visitors asked the master to discuss the concepts of paradise and purgatory. "These are not concepts!", exclaimed the master. "Paradise is as real as you and me and it's there for all to see and to experience."

"Then, how come we don't see it?, asked one of the students rather petulantly.

"It's because, most of the time, we live in purgatory", replied the master.

Prayers

The master was not what you would call a religious man. "Master", I asked once, "you taught me mantrams and you showed me paths in meditation, but you never taught me any prayers. Is there no use for them?"

"Of course there is", answered after a while the master. "Only, you have to find your own reasons for praying and then you will also know your prayers."

"Do you pray, master?"

"Yes. I do."

"What are your prayers about, if you don't mind me asking?"

"I salute the sun, shout my thanks to the stars, and ask for mercy from everything I eat and every plant I collect for my medicines. What else is there?"

God and love

The master very rarely, if ever, used the words 'god' and 'love', which he thought were the most misapprehended and misapplied words in the human vocabulary.

The nature of the universe

A student visitor asked the master about the nature of the universe. The master answered: "Yes!"

The student waited for more, but the master had gone back to quietly enjoying his tea.

"Is that all?", asked the student. "Won't you tell us more?"

"How do you expect to understand the nature of the universe with more words", said the master, "when you do not understand with just one?"

Questions

Once, the master accepted a question–and–answer session with a bunch of visiting students. They assured him they had pondered seriously upon their questions before coming to him. The master told them to go ahead.
"What is the greatest force in the universe?"
"Life."
"What is the greatest power available to man?"
"Faith."
"What is man's greatest weakness?"
"The mind."
"What is man's greatest illusion?"
"The self."
"What is man's greatest enemy?"
"Himself."
"What is man's greatest fear?"
"Death."
"What is man's purpose in life?"
"I thought this was going to be a serious questions session", said the master and refused to answer any more.

Ghosts

In a discussion about metaphysical creatures, the master dismissed everything as mythology, except, he said, for ghosts. Ghosts were very real.
We just sat there, staring at the master in confusion. Nobody had anything to say, or the courage to challenge the master for an explanation. "Come on!", said the master. "Ghosts! Can't you see them? All fantasies people harbour are feeding on them!"

Science

A student visitor asked the master his opinion about the sciences. He was a student of Physics himself, and talked about it with great fervor. "It's spirituality without the need for a God", he said at some point.

"It seems to me", said the master, "that your science, in trying to avoid seeing God *behind* everything, misses the chance to see God *in* everything."

Technology

About post–electricity technology, the master was also very forward. "Technology", he would say, "was the dream of yesterday; it is the force of today; and it will be the regret of all times."

Explaining away

"Why am I feeling so poorly, master? It must have been something I ate", I said, frowning in discomfort.
"You just explained away a perfectly legitimate and very important question", said the master.

Illumination

"I didn't see it coming", I said to the master, explaining the feeling I had about a sudden illumination during meditation, which had instantly disappeared, leaving behind it just a shadow.

"You saw it going", said the master, "which is better than not having seeing it at all."

Discovering

The master had come upon a cartoon strip called Calvin and Hobbes, drawn by the American artist Bill Watterson. He liked the particular strip so much, he made a story out of it:

A monk was digging in the monastery garden, using only his hands, when a wandering tourist hovered over him and watched with great curiosity.
"Did you find anything interesting?, asked the tourist.
"Yes!", said the monk excitedly. "I found two fat worms, a broken button and an ancient–looking plastic lighter!"
"Oh!", said the tourist.
"I know!", said the monk joyfully. "There's treasure everywhere!"

Now

"I have this uneasy feeling that I needed to do something which I forgot", I said to the master.
"Do you need to do something now?", he asked.
"No, no. I don't need to do anything right now."
"All time is right now", said the master.

Poor gains

A man from the nearby town came to the master, seeking advice on a problem he had with his brother. Their father had died and had left a house; regrettably, without leaving a will. The man's brother claimed that the house should be his, since he was the one who cared for their father in his final days. Was there a just solution to this problem that would also end the conflict with his brother? – the man wanted to know.

"Do you have a house to live?", asked the master.

"Yes. I have my own house and so does my brother", said the man.

"Do you have another brother or a sister?", asked again the master.

"No. He is the only one", said the man.

"Then it should be obvious to you that you should let your brother have the house. This would end the conflict immediately."

"Why?", said the man and his eyebrows almost joined in the middle. "Why should it be me who waives his right? By the same logic, my brother should also do the same."

"I agree!", said the master. "This would be a very enlightened response for both of you. However, your brother didn't come to me for advice; you did."

"And if he were here instead of me, what would you say

to him?", insisted the man, clearly not satisfied with the master's advice.

"I would tell him that if he went ahead with his demand, he would end up half a house richer and one brother poorer", said the master. "A brainless exchange, if you ask me", he concluded.

Desire

The master insisted that every time we sensed a desire forming inside us, regardless of its nature, we should always meditate on it before taking any action. "Desires are like beasts", he would say, "and man is full of them. Feed one, and you'll soon have to feed the lot."

Friendship

The master referred to us all as "my friends". Truth is, he valued friendship more than any other human bond. "In no other freely chosen relationship between humans can be found so many delicate and unspoken agreements that are followed to the letter", he once said.

Expectation

"Are you expecting rain, master?", I asked when I saw him covering the firewood and collecting the pillows from the benches in the yard.

"If you expect it, it doesn't come", replied the master. "I need rain, though, therefore I'm preparing for it."

Crime

One of the young fellows who gathered around the master when he was at home, was caught stealing in the nearby town and was punished for it by the authorities. Nevertheless, he showed up again at the house, and the master was glad to see him. He sat him next to him and served him tea himself. When someone, somewhat crossly, reminded the master that the boy was a thief, the master did not say anything. A few days later, the same person brought up the subject again, and again the following days, until the master finally responded. "He committed the crime once and he was punished for it", he said. "You, on the other hand; you commit the crime again and again, everytime you mention it."

Justice

"They say King Solomon of the Jews was a very wise and just man", said the master one day, "but if two women come to you, both claiming to be the mother of a baby, don't try any tricks. Assign the baby to both of them and hold them equally responsible for the welfare and the correct upbringing of the child."

Communication

"Master! Did I just see you talk to that bird?"
"Don't be silly", said the master, "how would the bird understand if I talked to it? I was singing to it, that's what I was doing."

Knowing

"I want to leave", said a young follower to the master.

"Yes", replied the master.

"What? Are you not going to stop me?"

"How could I?", asked the master.

"Well… By reminding me of the teachings, maybe, or by a binding order."

"Why should I?", asked again the master.

"Well… I don't know…", said somewhat unsure the young fellow.

"Then, maybe, you shouldn't leave", said the master and poured him some tea.

According to plan

"Master! You have got to come out of meditation! The young disciples are leaving, the granary is empty, there's no one to tend the field, and even the oil lamps will eventually stop burning in your master's shrine!"

The master came slowly out of meditation. "Relax", he said calmly. "Everything is going according to plan."

He then rested again in contemplation.

The way

We were parting, and I had one last question for the master: I asked if the way he showed me had a name, whereby without delay he slapped me hard in the face. Instantly, I knew what the name of the way was. I hugged him in affection and boarded my bus.

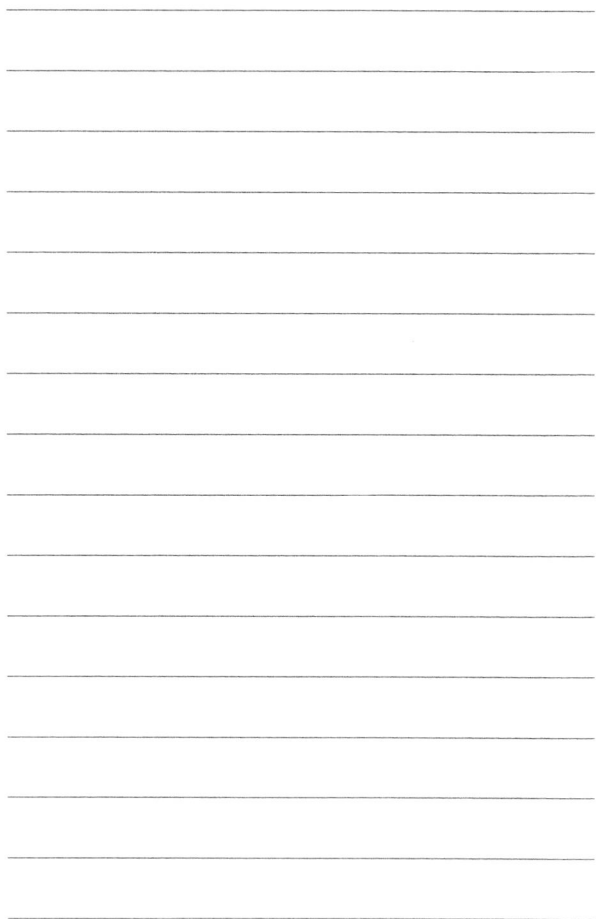

THIS BOOK IS SET

IN TIMES NEW ROMAN

AND IT WAS

DESIGNED AND ILLUSTRATED

BY THE AUTHOR

IN OCTOBER 2013

www.ingramcontent.com/pod-product-compliance
Lightning Source LLC
Chambersburg PA
CBHW071932020426

42331CB00010B/2830